Nights of *Fire, Nights* of *Rain*

Nights of Fire, Nights of Rain

Amy Uyematsu

Story Line Press, 1998

Published by: Story Line Press
             Three Oaks Farm
             Brownsville, Oregon 97327

This publication was made possible thanks in part to the generous support of the Nicholas Roerich Museum, the San Francisco Foundation, the Oregon Arts Commission, the Charles Schwab Corporation Foundation, and our individual contributors.

Book design by Stacy Rathbun
Cover design and artwork by Mary Kao

Library of Congress Cataloging-in-Publication Data
Uyematsu, Amy
    Night of Fire, Nights of Rain / Amy Uyematsu.
    p. cm.
    ISBN 1-885266-52-9
    1. City and town life—California—Los Angeles—Poetry.
2. Japanese Americans—California—Los Angeles—Poetry. 3. Los
Angeles (Calif.)—Poetry. I. Title.
PS3571.Y66N5 1998   97-40146
811'.54--dc21   CIP

Acknowledgements

I have had the good fortune to have many poet guides on my journey. Included among these are Momoko Iko, Florence Weinberger, Nels Christianson, Sesshu Foster, Ann Colburn, Karen Holden, Eric Chock, Mary Lee Gowland, Nancy Padron, Helen Friedland, Lee McCarthy, Joseph Bruchac, Joyce Nako, Russell Leong, and many more.

I also owe so much to family and friends who have supported my writing efforts—particularly my mother Elsie, sister Mary, Naomi Hirahara, Linda Rasmussen, and Miyo Tachiki for their extra support with 30 *Miles from J-Town*, and the ongoing encouragement, laughter, and nudges of Raul Contreras.

Still, it is with deepest gratitude that I have studied with Peter Levitt ("old father"), whose teachings about poetry, Zen, and intimacy with/in the world give such tenderly brilliant light. In ways I've learned to trust and just begun to understand, Peter is helping me to come home.

In addition, grateful acknowledgement is made to the following journals and anthologies in which some of these poems first appeared:

Amerasia Journal, Asian American Literary Realm, Asian Pacific American Journal, Bamboo Ridge Journal, Blue Mesa Review, Contact II, Crab Orchard Review, Daybreak, Dis/Orient, Flash Bopp, Forkroads, Mildred, The Phoenix, Pivot, Poetry/LA, Rafu Shimpo, Sister Stew, Solo, Tsunami, and *West/Word.*

Table of Contents

I

II

III

IV

TO

Chris and Raul

I.

The sound of gunfire

can go straight to the heart

of our intimacy.

—Roberto Sosa,
"Those the Violence Selects"

This Shame Called Joy
—for Thylias Moss

Hand squeezed,
thick with a pulp which clings
to this cup as I tilt it
slowly toward my mouth,
savoring the flesh, sweet
skin against skin—
orange juice.

But I need more assurance
for such small, deliberate joys.
I can't stop seeing
the tape of young Latasha Harlins
being shot in the back over a $1.79
carton of orange juice.
The grocer who kills Latasha
doesn't go to jail and I
can't convince anyone of the crime.
Or of my own outrage.

My senses grow darker each day.
This lust I cultivate for the ordinary,
the juice of an orange tasting more exquisite
than I ever remember,
cannot be separated from the brutal
death of a child who only wanted
to drink from the same fruit.

I need to acknowledge
my longing and hold joy on my tongue,
this desperate, glorious hunger
to take the whole world in—
even in its meanness—
for whatever it's willing to give.
Let me be grateful for
the tenacity of my desire.

Summons

we say we aren't the believers
but we won't leave the burning cities
we still think it's possible
to die peacefully in our sleep
even now when we have to train ourselves
to laugh out loud in our dreams
we pray for the gift of indifference
let it take over so slowly
we won't feel the narcosis sneak in
it won't depend on one catastrophe too much
and we can still be amazed at how easily
the brain protects us
from this knowledge our eye brings to the heart
tricking us into another good night's sleep
as we gather around the corpses
making sure we can't identify them

we take up gambling in a serious way
become more superstitious
reminded how rats in a maze get riled up
when there's a full moon
we do anything to better our odds
pay attention to all the warnings
don't go to bed with open windows
inhale in half breaths
consider sex with new lovers
a dangerous political act
we go to murderous lengths
to maintain a small semblance of order

we don't have to be threatened
lined up against the wall and blindfolded
we know what it feels like to wait

for that random bullet
aimed into the crowd for the sheer pleasure
and power of its anonymity

yes we cheer when it misses us
we lock our children indoors
while watching the neighborhood kids
gun each other down

we have never laughed harder for our good luck
no more talk about the end of the planet
we refuse to take anything too seriously
instead we'll hire troops of clowns
to travel throughout the empire
pay them good money to keep us laughing

we'll breathe just a little harder in our sleep
but we can endure anything
even will the victims' faces
right out of our dreams

Florentino Diaz

Has already figured out
that life is nothing more
than getting high
and getting laid
at 16 he doesn't ask anyone
for trouble
was just standing around
with his homeboys
when he got shot
nothing too serious
only a week in the hospital.

When Tino came back to school
it took only one day
to get himself hit in the face
and nobody has heard from him since.

I miss the sheepish grin
he brought into my classroom
his tall, gangling body
the way he slouched in hallways
holding his ground in a proud
pachuco tradition, that slight upward
turn of his chin, to show everyone
how little he cares.

The woman I eat lunch with,
known for her keen sense of humor,
has had it with spray paint,
carved initials, baggy trousers
which hang low on the hips,

lately she calls every Tino
nothing but a piece of shit
says they should all be sent back
if they refuse to fit in.

On Tino's last day at school
he gave me that sideways glance
barely raising his eyebrows
so only I could detect
a greeting nobody else could see.

What More

first we allow
the taking of children

children who live
in our vacant houses
jamming metal and scream
into life-size dolls

and the children we take
inside our own homes
who we watch
through cameras
as they line up
on asphalt and grass
scratching the ground
for bullets, a river,
pale ears for a necklace

on soweto streets
slender limbs are hurled
against walls
encrusted with glass and blood
but at night
these children grow new arms
hold each other in sleep
wonder
what more can be taken

Lessons from Central America

Always start with the male children.

Give them candy, Coca Cola, and guns.

Tell them secrets.
Teach them to doubt everything,
especially fathers and priests.
Show them what happens to men
who won't listen to reason
and necessity.

Take them to the grave of warm skulls.
Make them watch all the ways
for torturing a sister.

Do not trust them
too long with their mothers,
but do give them bread
and shoes for their feet.

Four Haiku (After Talking with David)

It begins here—
young men vanish in the night,
poets go to jail.

...

You lay down your brush,
it bleeds now from mouth to hand.
I fear what we know.

...

Girl, make up your mind—
a bird rests on soldier's gun.
Don't you hear one sound?

...

The night breathes out stars
so a man can carve new eyes—
it commands no one.

Early Morning in Midtown

You can't get me
I won't look inside this bag
laid out on these jagged steps
like a subway dare
I know there's a man
inside who breathes
and hears me walking by
I won't let myself
stop
even if I already see
how tall you are
how many stairs I must climb
to pass the length of your body
but you can't get me
I won't slow down
why should I when everyone
behind pushes me forward

Don't you understand
I can't do anything
besides who in their right mind
would choose to sleep on this
incline of cold cement
why don't you burrow
like the others
against the dark
subterranean walls

Why don't you get up and walk
look me in the eyes
as defiant as the others
ask me for change

You think you've got me
but I'll show you
I don't even care enough
to check your face
for signs of life
I don't want to know
if you lie under your blanket
eyes unable to close
waiting for a city
of footsteps to rush
by without speaking
wave after wave

Don't you get it
even if I try to stop
I'll get trampled
so I've already forgotten you
won't remember anything
by tomorrow morning

No, you can't get me.

Storm

it's been raining for hours
water endlessly draining
through the tiny gutters
which surround my head
I welcome the whine of a police siren
or car wheels splashing an exit
on the wet streets below

> I've heard twenty men with twenty drums
> imitate rain
> not the quiet kind
> but the hard, relentless clatter
> striking a tin roof
> a rain to stop everyone from sleeping

when the storm clears the day
is too blue and warm for winter
those of us who look up to the sky
cannot take our eyes from the strange
cloud with no roundness
as if painted in one sure sweep
of a careful hand
all day this cloud hangs over our heads
even the wind cannot move it

> I've seen the wind
> take blue out of the sky
> cover an entire city with grey
> ash in the air rains on all of us
> our skin stinking of soot
> for days we try washing
> our bodies clean

at night the sky empties to no stars
no voice answering back
it's as if everyone has vanished
all these houses whose beds are still warm
out of the silence a twig snaps
then walls vibrate
to the stampede of heavy feet
growing in the dark

Dreaming of Fire on the Night It Rained

I am trapped in a house owned by strangers with white skin. I do not like it here but know I can't leave. Fires are burning throughout the city. Though new fires break out randomly, the timing between each new outburst is almost rhythmic. Everyone waits in expectation for the next one. The flames get closer to this old frame house. I am only nine or ten but try to convince the white man who owns the house that it needs to be hosed down with water. He ignores me. So I search outside and find a short hose. The water pressure is low but I manage to get a small stream, which I aim toward the roof and to the building's sides. Some parts of the wooden structure are so weak they break under the slightest pressure of the water. The white strangers in the house frighten me but I know my fate is tied to them. I must keep watering the dry, dry wood. For now it is all I can do.

In America Yellow Is Still an Insult

1

I want to know why cowards are called yellow.
I've seen a few in my time with their ghostwhite skin.
Who named journalism yellow when it reached new lows,
and when did union traitors turn
into yellow dogs?

2

She says she won't wear amber, her birthstone.
Does its yellow remind her more of the shade of piss
than gold, a ripe lemon, or those famous fields of grain?
Is it the yellowish-green discoloration
in newborns endangered with jaundice?
Statistics back up her dislike,
yellow the least preferred of all
primary colors.

3

Immunize against
Hong Kong flu #5,
even more deadly
than last year's
Asian viral strain #44C,
microscopic infestations
of the latest yellow peril,
too many boatloads
and planefuls to stop.

Symptom:
Asians are the fastest growing
population in California.

4

You can't even imagine being me, a yellow-skinned man.
Instant caricature.
Nameless slant-eyed enemy with kamikaze mentality.
Devious as Charlie Chan and his Karate Kid counterpart.
I'm Jerry Lewis on Saturday morning cartoons,
all bucktoothed and singsong incomprehensible.
College nerd with no testosterone.
Grinning, squinting businessman
always dressed in the same dark suit and camera.
I'm cast as the voiceless boyfriend
who deserves to lose lovely Asian to big, brave Anglo,
I play the cowering eunuch
who stars in no women's fantasies.
Just try to be a real yellow man in America
and know the legacy of insult.

Someone Is Trying to Warn You
— "Your Boss May Be Japanese,"
Newsweek cover story, 1/87

And the whole world is talking about the Japanese
who buy up America, collecting skyscrapers
like so many red & green plastic Monopoly pieces.
You're part of some new financial game,
only you don't make the rules anymore—
"Made in Japan" used to be your joke
until too many factory towns shut down.
Now runaway shops are coming back home
and they're hiring *you* as cheap foreign labor.
America's a country ripe for the taking
by these little yellow men who all look the same
in their dark business suits and menacing smiles—
a bargain investment for Japanese yen.

Lately all you see are slanted eyes,
newcomers who may as well be Japanese
even when you know we're not.
No matter if we talk in many languages,
live in separate sections of the city,
arrived last year or a century earlier.
No difference
if we don't get along with each other
or speak perfect English—
you can't help mixing us up
because we all work so hard,
buy restaurants and small businesses,
know how to save money and steadily
take over your neighborhoods,
ace out you and your kids
for the best grades and jobs.

Even you can admit some admiration
though never sure of our next move—
you'll always mistrust us for the shape of our eyes,
narrow and devious like Fu Manchu,
Ho Chi Minh, unstoppable kamikaze pilots,
only you're more nervous this time—
you see us invading without firing a shot—
Japanese businessmen zeroing in on downtown Los Angeles,
Korean shopkeepers spreading along Olympic & Western,
Chinese immigrants pushing you out of Monterey Park,
running for Mayor, sneaking past the once untouchable
borders of lily-white San Marino,
Pilipino families buying West Valley tract homes,
Hmong refugees getting welfare,
Vietnamese students winning spelling bees,
going to Harvard and West Point,
young Asian hoodlums topping the evening news
broadcast by Tritia Toyota and Connie Chung lookalikes.

You blame us for all the overseas cars and TV's
you keep buying—it's our fault you're unpatriotic—
seducing you for paychecks, even taste buds,
as you quickly learn to distinguish pad Thai
noodles from won ton, kim chee, miso shiro soup.
You can't keep us silent like the old days,
as we demand apologies and reparations
for locking up 110,000 Japanese Americans in 1942.
You're unable to stop us from over-
populating the best universities,
marrying your sisters and daughters.
And though you won't say this publicly,
you fear Pearl Harbor is repeating itself—
only there are too many of us this time,
the ashes of Hiroshima, Seoul, and Saigon still warm,
you still haven't won the war.

Greeting
— Jackson Hole, Wyoming, 1992

The boy with yellow hair
and sky-colored eyes
stops when he sees me,
a certain authority and too familiar smile
growing in his small, pale face,
pleased as he calls out, "Tonto."

Lexicon

try not to be insulted
when they call us oriental.
let exotic be a compliment.
even the most educated among them
will ask how long we've been here,
be genuinely surprised we speak English so well.
don't expect other wrongnamed people to be any better.
immigrants from Guatemala and Mexico
will keep calling us Chino,
even when we explain we were born here.
"you know what we mean," they'll say,
and we'll tell them our parents were born here too.
"you know what we mean," they'll insist,
so we'll tell them our grandparents came from Japan.
they'll nod their heads,
still calling us Chino when they talk among themselves.
don't let these daily misunderstandings get to you.

learn how to differentiate.
slanted eyes is o.k.
but not you slanteyes, tighteyes, sliteyes, zipperheads.
to most of them Jap, Chink, or Gook all mean the same.
don't let them tell us that "kill
the fuckin Gook," spoken in combat,
is separate from "too many Chinks moving in"
to Anaheim, California, or Biloxi, Mississippi.
watch the mouth and eyes carefully as they say the words.
maybe our closest friends can call us crazy Japs,
but be cautious when their talk turns
to those sneaky Japs who attacked Pearl Harbor,
who deserved to be put away in camps,
bombed at Hiroshima and Nagasaki.

pay close attention to headlines
which warn about "influx," "imbalance," "invasion."
don't consider any place safe anymore.
watch what they hide in their hands.
in Raleigh, North Carolina, Ming Hai Loo
was gunned down by two brothers
who hated Vietnamese. Loo was Chinese.
and it didn't matter if Vincent Chin
was clubbed to death
by two Detroit autoworkers
who mistook him for Japanese.

don't expect them to ask us our real names.
don't even try.

Border Tallies

still climbing gold mountain

it's a little known fact
that we're the fastest growing
American minority

by 2050 Asians will be 10 percent

no accident
when I'm stopped
twice in a row
by the U.S. patrol
between Vancouver and Seattle
grilled again
coming back from Quebec

my dad and his new Pilipino wife
finally return from Toronto
after several attempts
telling the Detroit official
they only want
to spend the day
at a local mall

they live in a gated community
of 9000 seniors
less than 90 nonwhite
not a single black
they've heard it's too dangerous
to walk at a nearby beach
where Vietnamese get jumped
one even beaten to death

meanwhile the real gold rush is on

in Shanghai young blue-eyed prospectors
comb the narrow streets
checking the shelves
of shop after shop
to see how many
are stocked with Skippy
and other common household names

1.2 billion peanut butter sandwiches

tonight on television a camera
zooms in on a stack of Crest toothpaste
its familiar U.S. logo
also translated
in smaller Chinese characters

1.2 billion sets of teeth to shine

The Ten Million Flames of Los Angeles
—a New Year's poem, 1994

I've always been afraid of death by fire,
I am eight or nine when I see the remnants of a cross
burning on the Jacobs' front lawn,
seventeen when Watts explodes in '65,
forty-four when Watts blazes again in 1992.
For days the sky scatters soot and ash which cling to my skin,
the smell of burning metal everywhere. And I recall
James Baldwin's warning about the fire next time.

> *Fires keep burning in my city of the angels,*
> *from South Central to Hollywood,*
> *burn, baby, burn.*

In '93 LA's Santana winds incinerate Laguna and Malibu.
Once the firestorm begins, wind and heat regenerate
on their own, unleashing a fury so unforgiving
it must be a warning from the gods.

> *Fires keep burning in my city of the angels,*
> *how many does it take,*
> *burn, LA, burn.*

Everybody says we're all going to hell.
No home safe
from any tagger, gangster, carjacker, neighbor.
LA gets meaner by the minute
as we turn our backs
on another generation of young men,
become too used to this condition
of children killing children.
I wonder who to fear more.

Fires keep burning in my city of angels,
but I hear someone whisper,
"Mi angelita, come closer."

Though I ready myself for the next conflagration,
I feel myself giving in to something I can't name.
I smile more at strangers, leave big tips to waitresses,
laugh when I'm stuck on the freeway, content
just listening to B.B. King's "Why I Sing the Blues."

"Mi angelita, mi angelita."

I'm starting to believe in a flame
which tries to breathe in each of us.
I see young Chicanos fasting one more day
in a hunger strike for education,
read about gang members preaching peace in the 'hood,
hear Reginald Denny forgiving the men
who nearly beat him to death.
I look at people I know, as if for the first time,
sure that some are angels. I like the unlikeliness
of this unhandsome crew—the men losing their hair,
needing a shave, those with dark shining
eyes, and the grey-haired women, rage
and grace in each sturdy step.
What is this fire I feel, this fire which breathes freely
inside without burning them alive?

Fires keep burning in my city of angels,
but someone calls to me,
"Angelita, do not run from the flame."

II.

I say hello to those

who came before me.

—Linda Hogan, "First Light"

To Talk about a River

i

I remember a time before speaking.
A memory of the wet
skin covering eye, of wind and fingers,
and a river with no name.
Then a voice calls me, just beyond
the sound of black water.

It gets quiet again.
I move my hands slowly in the dark.
These walls are cool, damp cave.
Water lays hidden within.
Filaments become visible
in the afternoon light.
Tendrils finer than infant hair,
suspended from the dome,
delicate threads carrying buds
of rain—each moist bead
a different name, sounded again and again,
then takes to the air on its own.

ii

But this is what we are.
We bring fire to see the pictures
and greetings left behind.
For others to know.
Once we climbed out of the river
and felt our separation.
Now we go back and sing it our names,
sometimes fashion a sound
so we are almost a river—
a river that never knew we left it.

Bone Flute

first there were flutes & drums
to accompany the known sounds—
    a mother's heartbeat   her lover's moan
    infant cry   and a fisherman's gasp

      our chanting which came before spoken song

in every tribe if one child was born
with no eyes   or when an old woman
forgot why she wanted to talk

      we carved them flutes
      from ivory, birdbone, fruitshell, clay
      smooth and light in the hand

      these magic sticks could bring fertility
      and those lucky enough to feed them melody
          were said to be charmed

once a boy heard his breath
through a willow/his sister
whistled through the curved
bone of a deer

      we took these sounds as our own,
      that other creatures would know us
          as human

on the eight islands east of China
flutemakers wore rope sandals   straw baskets
                on their heads   wide brims shading eyes
                so we would know them only by their music

        they became wandering priests
        we can still hear their shakuhachi—

        the long breath through
                        thick bamboo reed   as we enter
        this common memory of light and wind
                        pressing the dark hollow

                each tone overlapping to fill out a world,
                the moist and endless vibration
                                from one low quiver rising.

shakuhachi: Japanese bamboo flute

The Calligrapher

He stoops on the sandy ground,
feet hidden by weeds, wearing
the loose cotton jacket of foreigners,
this solitary man
as he brushes names in black ink
with his light, swift hand,
ancient Chinese characters crowding
picture and story onto tall stone markers,
names now confined to outskirts
of the young city.
Behind him jagged rocks
form the mountain's base:
these are the stones
trapped in the belly of Gold Mountain,
these ghosts who left
no wives or children,
these ghosts in loose jackets
who came to California
and never went back.

The Well

Imagine a mountain whose name is heart.

At the throat of the mountain
they fill a well
with so many stones
it can hold nothing more.

They'd never heard of
the mountain named heart,
Kokoro-yama, til they were taken
as prisoners to Heart Mountain.

Imagine a heart big enough to be called mountain.

A mound of stones,
too many to count, remain—
each inscribed
by a different hand,
each crying out.

Some simply reveal
the writer's name—
Shizuko, a woman,
or a family known as Osajima.
Most of the handpainted
rocks carry a single kanji—
snow   wind   cold   sky
shame   home   bird.

—for the 12,000 Japanese Americans
    interned at Heart Mountain, Wyoming

Wind River

It is just a matter of relocation
one jail or the next
for men from the reservation
the first young man
hanged himself
then more began to die
a few friends
some chose guns
then others who had only heard
the story of the first man.

When he was just born
his grandmother cradled him
in her arms
whispering the knowledge
of their tribe
she passed him among the circle of women
or carried him on her back
in the old way
he learned the stories
in words he can't say
to pass on.

Then she talked to him
from another place
after the bitter liquids
she comes to him as he sleeps
I will take you to the America undreamed
I will show you
how to dance
to the tapping of rain
ride wind
on the middle plain
recite the names
of your fathers' mothers
to the stars.

Note: Based on the deaths of nine young men in the fall
of 1985, near the Wind River Reservation, Wyoming.

Corn Seed

This angle of moon
through my side window
unravels its light
like a fine bone gauze,
settles along the north wall
until it touches her photograph—
the tribeswoman
with long braided hair,
who answers to many names.
My eyes grow steady within
the room's darkness where
she waits to be revealed
in shadow, linking us
cheekbone and skin,
our color deepened like earth
yellow to red to brown,
the dark skin toughens,
protects us from sun
and the long separation
from hands far outside us.

But her eyes looking out
with no bitterness,
despite all she has seen—
not from this time
when we've started to rave
in the familiar
dreaming of victims,
only louder as we pass
the resharpened arrow
between hand and tongue.

Now when there is so much anger
in us, I return here—
where I can see through
one tribeswoman's eyes,
after she has watched her sons die.
I hear the rhythm of her
plow and loom,
preparing the ground
for corn seed,
laying out new blankets,
bright winter wool.
Though she awakens
again among warriors,
it is her voice—in light
repetition of water on stone,
a woman who bends shadow,
teaching me how to rename
things at night.

Sitting before her
with my child's bold stare,
I ask about defending our
dignity—but she laughs,
tells me I come from a village
by the sea. She knows
I am called growing pine tree.
Then we greet each other,
this old woman and me,
while we listen to
all the movement in my house.

Witness

—from a painting of abandoned baby carriages near
Terezin Concentration Camp, Czech Republic

The first time I looked up
and saw the sky had her face,
my eyes became comfortable
in that light, new eyes
that still didn't know
my face separate
from hers.

But the sky changed.
A tree fills the space once owned by her.
I hear my name—
no human eyes gaze back at me now,
only these tall winter trees
know how much I was loved.

A Long Way from Here
—after seeing "Salaam Bombay"

Two boys sleep
by the trunk of a banyan tree
their dark arms tangled,
legs bent at odd
angles, bones
protruding at knees,
shoulder blades
and ribs, the smaller
child folded like extra skin
on the older boy's belly
and chest—
they are not lovers
though no love could go further.

When the city is finally quiet
two boys return
to this tree, grateful
for a day like no other,
enough money for cigarettes
and a bit of hashish.

Under a starlit sky they
talk about going
home someday,
fall asleep in each other's arms,
lightheaded and full.

Even After She Leaves

—for my mother

Light has been carried into this house
carefully rearranged
with an insistence—
walls pushed out
wider windows cut
no darkened hallways
no secrets tucked into pillows
or hurried into phone conversations.

There is evidence of small hands—

In the tiny clay tiles
set one by one onto a coffee table.
Sometimes a snake
patterned from domino blocks
winds slowly across,
then one press of a finger,
black and white clicking
against the glazed red top.

Or the lid removed
from a round lacquer bowl,
deep enough for all the jewelry
which can't be thrown away—
the loose pearls which slide
from broken strings
pins with missing rhinestones
matching brass buttons
snipped from a green velvet coat,
each to be pieced back together
like fragments of story.

It's the way light can move
in some hands—
a corner chosen
so a Japanese scroll
reflects late afternoon—
pale moss for its wide silk border
and a center the color of bone,
lines and lines of ink—
brushed names
being called out in silence.

An intentional light
held with the practiced touch
of a still beautiful woman
who studies her face in the mirror,
knows each shadow and angle,
remembers the best time for gathering sun.

There is evidence of hands
no longer smooth—

Floors scraped and varnished
down to their bare skin,
now that time has an older sound
soft as wool socks
padding rhythm
into the cool blond wood.

In her kitchen the smell
of fresh dirt on green beans,
the cucumbers just picked,
sliced thin and tasted
in light crunching sounds—
and these eggshells
collected in a blue enamel dish,
waiting to be fed back
to the same dark soil.

Alone with the Old Farmer's Wife

shoes:

by the doorway I hear him
step out of his shoes
he makes no sound
as he enters the unlit room
stands in the dark
for a long time
the earthen floor
under his bare feet
before calling to me
'I'm home'

rice:

these three kitchen pots
can tell anyone
about us
the sturdiest container
kept warm all day
enough rice for every meal
a second pan for stirring tofu
onions and greens
then a small one for soup
its metal still shiny
after all these years
even when empty
the ladle rests inside
ready to pour
the next steaming broth

newspaper:

sometimes I forget how long
and black my hair was
now I keep it hidden
in a bandana
no longer bothering
to remove the scarf
when I return from the fields

I used to hurry back
before fixing supper
wash the dirt off my face and hands
loosen my hair
brushing until it lay full
and glistening on my back
the way he liked it
I don't remember when
he stopped sliding his fingers
through my hair
he didn't say anything
the year I cut it

now I give myself more time
sit down on the floor
and lay out today's paper
my hair still tucked
in its cotton bandana
taking in all
that's new in the world

prayer:

every night I pray
to my small shrine
the statue so faded and chipped
paint on the head and shoulders
worn to brown clay
yet a smile remains
and the ancient robe opens
to a huge round belly

before this ragged god I place
fresh flowers every week
and next to the bowl
offering fruit
or sweet rice
I bring tea

wood:

I stop to look at the yard
admiring the way he
arranges the tools
neatly along one wall
firewood piled high
with logs stacked small to large
but I am the one
who insists on planting
this cherry tree
so its trunk leans
toward the horizon
the dark stem
slanting
between sky and ground
its branches still widening
to hold
each blossom

The Bachelor's Unwritten Letter to Japan

The old man feels lucky tonight.
He just came home with the freshest
mackerel from Iwamoto's stand.
He salts the fish and sets his small
table as if there'll be guests,
carefully arranging the pot
of steaming rice, a large bottle
brimming with warm sake,
the just opened jar of spring
cabbage pickled by Yoshi's wife.

It is late summer and he'll eat until full,
lingering under this San Joaquin moon—
its slow light crossing the infinite
lines of sugar beets, lettuce, and
peas which furrow
through the dark to his home.

III.

Like the bloodheart tree

outside your window our own hearts

become known to us.

—Karen Holden,
"The Bloodheart Tree"

Fish

I enter
to know the sound
of my mother's breathing
and the waters
which cradle me.

In so little time
I have already claimed
this separate eye,
given names to what
appears visible to me
within its half
perimeter,
though it floats on
a surface of sea tears,
it runs the width
of my dreams.

Before the written word
what was the sound
leading to "I"?
In my own ancient tongue
the same sound "ai"
signals the cool blue
center of a morning glory,
that deep indigo
surrounding the islands
where my ancestors fished,
and "ai" means love
in Japanese
but is hardly spoken
out loud.

A Woman Named Matsu/Pine

—after seeing decorated pine cones on
   Shinto shrines, Kyoto, 1983

I wait here before our children
awake, light turning

beneath a forest of pine,
the sea mist opens and closes

around me, salt and night
mountain memory moisten

my skin. From the damp
ground I uncover

the sturdiest pine cone,
dress it in fabric and bead,

a red scarf on its head,
then place my small token

on this ancestral shrine.
From layers of needles

I braid pine into rope,
my arms cradling

the fragrant wood
bundles—to bring back

fire in the dawn's
stillest hour.

By a Small River
—for Peter Levitt

1

A man chooses to build his house
near water, to sleep
with open windows and awaken
once more to the rhythms
of this small river :
home to the apple tree he plants here,
to his dog who catches the stones
he throws far beyond sight,
home to the child who swims naked
and invites him in.

2

Stopping by the river I
recognize you, an old man
who travels in straw sandals,
the same shakuhachi, eager
to strum a new tune.

3

You ask us to each call out
our own dark birth, to carry
the tangled roots to water.
We hear your quiet,
persistent singing as we pass
the small infant cord
between our hands,
stand together in
the rain and long after.

The Separation

Tonight I didn't expect that familiar pain
in my breasts, a fullness I used to feel
just before his next feeding—
only now my child is almost a man.

We argued and shouted again yesterday.
He said I don't listen to him,
accused me of not trusting what he says.
It's been a long time since he let himself
cry in front of me—
his tears came from a place only he could know,
the same way he cried when his father moved away,
back trembling like a small animal.
I was frightened.

When he was six he drew a picture of a desert—
there's an armadillo, a thin brown mouse,
bull with black horns, and a prehistoric dog that laughs.
One yellow striped snake wiggles
next to a horse with pink hair, and every cactus
stands sturdy with wide open arms.
The head of a rhinoceros peeks out behind a jagged cliff
while three birds keep rising into a white morning sky.
Though we had never been to this desert
my young child already knew its activity.

Later when I took him to a New Mexico desert,
he didn't want to draw. His teachers at school
had shown him what real art looks like,
and no matter what I said, he believed them.
Sometimes a mother turns her back
for only seconds—but her baby has already found matches,
been abducted by strangers. Now my son copies
dragons and airplanes from books and photographs,
and I know I am part of the betrayal.

The Woman Who Forgot

Sometimes a woman must go
a long way to remember
the real color of moon.
That summer she looked
in a southern country,
where the night sky
is too warm for clouds,
too black for stars.
She took her son, thinking
he would learn from this too.

It rained four times
the day they went to the jungle.
They passed through small
towns, on streets too low
for rivers of rain;
each time the sun
burned back in—
pavements steamed,
doors opened,
old men overheard.
When they reached Chichen-Itza,
the boy rushed
from pyramid to pyramid,
and the woman raced him,
pleased she could run
fast as a young boy.
The grass, greener
from the afternoon storm,
clung to their legs.

At night there was no rain,
the moon and sky contained
in one black forest.
The boy slept during their long
ride home, heard the moon
in his mother's voice.
But she had forgotten this.
So only the woman watched
the moon, her son by her side,
until she knew
she had never left it behind.

Mother's Day Poem to Myself

Your cord took ten days to fall off,
a tiny dry twig,
you didn't feel it breaking
away from your belly.
I barely remember
finding the shriveled stub,
almost unnoticed
in your bath water,
not knowing I'd want
to keep this as evidence,
this thread of skin
which grew in
my body—solely to feed you.
I should've saved our cord
in a small earthen jar,
kept it with a lock
of your hair,
so straight and black,
even at birth.
Did anyone warn me
there'll be weeks
I never hear your voice,
days even I no longer
wonder what you're doing?
How could I know that
mothers like me have only
eighteen years before we
finally feel the cut.

Son with Blue Shaven Head

—based on a Kunisada print

i

The woman who stands
in this river of dark blue,

her white hand
cupping the small

chin of the boy
she once nursed, does not know

he still watches her, his eyes
never leaving her face,

he wonders why she looks out
from the water

without him, long before
she takes her hand away.

ii

With one eye she looks out
from the water, her other eye

belongs to him, never
leaving his upturned head,

never too far from the river.

Who Have Been Sad
Even Before They Could Learn

Where do they come from—
these children with old faces,
no visible evidence of abuse or neglect.
Was it a conversation overheard in the womb?
Or merely an infant wanting to sleep on its back
while the mother turns it over and over on its belly.

I was one of those children who always looks
older than the rest.
A mystery to the others.
At eleven I remember talking with Merle McPheeters,
a grey-eyed boy who, with some admiration,
called me "sophisticated."
Merle said I didn't have to get silly like so many girls.
I couldn't explain yet how tired a young mouth can feel,
how languid the eyes, when
the world is faced, again and again,
with absolute seriousness.
That day Merle smiled as if imagining himself
too sophisticated for a small town preacher's son.
He couldn't have known how a random remark
from one kid to another
can last a girl her entire life.

To Get to the Child

I have to set just one man free—
the daddy I've held prisoner for over 40 years,
making sure he can never get away.
I feed him just enough,
nod my head like I always do
as he talks without blinking
or stopping to pause.
I punish him more by not letting him know
exactly what his crimes are.
I make very sure he never hears
my muffled sounds,
never notices these constant, tiny self
mutilations I inflict,
I inflict now, all by myself.

I Never Hear Myself Sleeping

never know what triggers
tooth against tooth
that grind
to wake everyone but me
unable to hold the noise
as the memory's slow
gnashing against itself
jars the darkness

when was the first time
my heart clasped
itself so hard
the charge pressed upward
past throat
but not tongue
leaving me wordless
and nervous
an unwelcome trait
passed from my father
the incisors
ready to devour

in whose unsuspecting
night ear
will I mouth
my contentment
to claw on raw gum
scrape bone against bone
my tiny jagged grin

A Father's Story

Each night the boy cries. The next morning a tiny white stone
appears by his bed. He doesn't know why but he senses he must
hide every trace of his suffering, so he hides the stone in
his pocket until he can go outside, and when nobody's watching,
throws the rock as far as it will fly. This goes on for one
thousand nights. Until the boy runs out of tears. Somehow he
survives, though his hands always feel cold. He's sure this
is how some men are born. He lives the best way he can,
marries, glad his own children are daughters. As he grows
old, he forgets the boy who cried.

Daughter's Song

I don't remember the touch of a father's hands.
This isn't possible.
In black and white photographs
he carries me in his arms.

It is easier for me to go looking for stones.
To take a small white pebble,
squeeze it in my hand,
like anger held tight in a young child's fist.
I think I hear the rush of water,
but what comes through its hardened surface
is the sound of a man's sadness
contained in my own.

If only I could grab that hand
which can't move toward me
even when it wants to.
Instead I keep stumbling on rocks, reminded
there's never much time.

Lately I lie awake in the dark,
the ordinary stone I've placed by my bed
glows with an unfamiliar warmth.
I cradle it in my hands,
skin pressed to stone,
turning it over and over as my hands
become moist, covered with tears
much older than my own.
When I see all the fathers born with no hands,
then I know I was the tiny stone my father hid
under his tongue and saved for me.
Somehow my hands became stronger
than his and I am a daughter who can
begin to love back, to give
one stone our name.

The Run

I enter again
                    through this sleeve
                                        of blue light
            water next to my feet

now when my legs
                    don't belong to my body
        and my breathing becomes quiet
                                effortless,
    all I can hear is the wind
                    low pitched and thick
                            like an old woman's song.

There is nobody here
                                only wind and sea
                    the salt of my own sweat
                    stinging my eyes

                            and I can't feel my feet
                                    remembering

        I was once a fish
                    waiting for the moon
                                know how its light
                            can penetrate water
                pulling me deeper.

It is slower   on the way back
            as if I am nothing
          more than pounding
                        legs and heart,

but I don't break my stride
                when a fisherman approaches
                    with blankets and poles
                ready to spend the night

                    he opens
        a thermos of coffee   fragrant and
                steaming into a sky
                        which darkens around us,

so dark he can't see me
                as I run past,   making no sound
                leaving only
                        this warm rush of air
                    here, close to the water's edge.

Belly Breaths

i

The belly of the world
is empty and round—
do you hear its noisy breathing
or its deep silent laugh?

ii

Inside the womb, a baby
and its mother breathe,
belly inside belly,
the world of the mother
so warm and wet,
long before new life
is forced out
into light,
to breathe on its own.

iii

It's in the hunger that we know who we are.

iv

In Japanese the word *kokoro*—
a tiny container for what can't possibly
be put into words—
mind / heart / spirit / idea / will / attention .

v

When was the last time
we laughed 'til our bellies ached?

vi

His belly full with mother's milk,
the baby can't help smiling in his sleep.

vii

Danger:
Don't forget to feed the imagination.

viii

Like a pine tree, grow
deep roots. Spread
branches thick with ever-
green, bring
breath close
to the core.

IV.

My own body spoke

from its long shyness.

—Patricia Hampl,
"An Artist Draws a Peach"

Where the Sky and Ground Are White
—from a Munakata painting

I press my lips together slightly,
purse them into the shape *mu*,
like the beginning of a kiss,
mu, the Japanese word for nothing.

Not knowing calligraphy,
I expect a simpler brush stroke,
the sparest of picture characters,
a thinner ink merging invisibly.
But *mu* is a house of thick,
black walls, where Munakata's hand
can still be felt, bold and rhythmic,
leaping out from the whiteness.

He lets me see my own dark
house—standing on four sturdy legs,
which could be stones
or the bodies I keep buried close by.
There are no obvious doors—
only tiny windows, rooms
remaining in shadow,
and outside a groundless sky.

I've slept many nights
but don't remember names and dates,
how I enter or leave, barely
a memory of belonging.
But there is something
in the way my house reveals
itself in shadow,
its darkness growing in the light.

There is something in the heart
of even one lone woman
which is too complex and impossible,
too furious to ignore.

Once

the moon and my body
kept the same blue rhythm.
I measured my pulse
from the tides.
The week before a reborn moon,
I felt my body yielding
to the gathering light,
a mother's unused body
filling with salt and water,
a sadness that connected me
to all things.

Now my blood comes more often,
the precious eggs break sooner,
as if the womb knows
it will soon be empty.
Lovers gather under the full moon
and so do old women, who sigh
their longing into the bleeding ground.

The Field I Stand Before

I spent so many years crouching
close to the ground—
planting seedlings of rice,
giving birth to children.
My legs grew sturdy.
I used to come home with mud on my hands.

Now I wake in upstairs bedrooms—
blood beneath nails, and air
thick with the smell of my own sex.
I have no memory of this hand
trying to hurtle me through dream,
a small palm pushing hard
against my unused womb,
fingering the crack,
searching for an opening
in this wet, sore skin.

To Women Who Sleep Alone

my mother doesn't understand a world with no man in it
tells me I waste too much time
forgets I used to spend hours playing by myself.

I don't tell her what sleeping alone is really like
the sweet oils no one but me can rub into my skin.
I look at my body again
no longer as pretty
all the young men I've sent away
will not be coming back.

lately my body's scent fills every room to smother me
I wonder if any man can still enjoy its taste
a darker odor.
every month my blood flows harder
an ache building within my thighs
a real part of me dying—
I want to let in the smell of trees and wind after it's rained.

there's a small grey bird outside my house
who keeps building
her nest with pine needles.
every evening the wind scatters her work
but she returns the next day with new twigs
determined to make a home here.

I'm not one of those women
who can make up their minds
just like that
to find a man again—
something my mother never taught me.
men have always come to me
asked me to dance
I'm not sure how to bring them back in.

sometimes I take a small branch of asparagus fern
twirl it around and around—
a light green fuzz powdering my arms.
then I curl my hands under my breasts
reassured by the softness of skin
remind myself this is enough for now—
my thin hand pausing on the shoji door
running my fingers along rice paper and wood—
a woman opening to the sound of rain.

Asian Zodiac

Love in the twelfth sign
can be dangerous—

Two wild boars,
we are born too close
keep crashing
against barriers
head first, roaring

We greet each other
too quickly
repeating this
history of children once
abandoned, always
this impatience
to be chosen

Even when love can begin
with arms tendered—
gifts of fern
and Hawaiian fish—
we still cannot stop
ourselves, charging
red-eyed
at some unseen
disturbance
always rushing
so surely
past our possibility.

With a Calligrapher

He writes every morning with a fat ink brush. His fingers slicing
the air, the faint swish on white paper. No movement wasted. His
posture, every long breath, all the days it's taken to reach this
effortlessness.

I watch his hands when he talks. He can flutter his fingers
like a hummingbird. The same way small finger puppets quiver
and hypnotize children. I imagine his supple hands touching
every part of me.

He likes being known for his hands. Cuts women's hair for a living.
His scissors merely an extension of his fingers. His body is so
thin. Women don't take him seriously.

He takes me out to dance flyaway Latin rhythms. We watch each
other, my feet not keeping time with his. I don't know what I really
want from him. But I need to be wanted again. Like he does.

Then one night we dance to a slow love song, he feels my breasts
against his chest, and everything changes for him—he'll tell me
this later. How he can think only of my breasts now. Sucks them
greedily. Asks me to bounce them for him as he lays beneath.
That merely watching me is enough.

He says we should spend more time together, but I need to know
he wants my Asian body. I remember he left Japan to live in
Europe. I know the women he dreams about—big-boned women
with mammoth white breasts, which he kneads over and over
in his hands.

And my desire? Is it only for his hands, for the way he can rub the
thick bristles of an ink brush in his fingers, press the fragrant wet
ink against each snow white sheet—no stroke repeated the same
way, each one becoming more his own. For just one night I want
all the power in his hands, which he holds onto with his life.

Five Nights of Rain

1

Open-throated,
wanting more.

2

We drive on the wet
road, wind and moon
breaking through.

3

Batter me hard,
strike my roof
like a drummer
who can't stop.

4

If I can fall asleep
to rain and wake
to its sound, why
won't it rain
in my dream?

5

Water coming
so loud no one can
hear me, so
relentless the rain.

Muchas Gracias

Just about everyone in California
knows the phrase, *"Muchas gracias"*—not just
thank you, but *muchas* for very much. I never
expected to find *"mucha"* in Japanese, which stretches
the meaning to so much more. It fits the way my life's
been going lately—*mucha*, defined as absurd, rash,
excessive, unreasonable, blindly or recklessly. And even
this doesn't go far enough. I had to smile when
I found *"mucha-kucha"* just below *mucha*
in my Japanese dictionary. It means exactly
how it sounds to my ears—confused, topsy-turvy,
madly, utterly making a mess of things—as in still
being in love with the wrong man,
muchas mucha-kucha.

Before Bruce Lee There Was Toshiro Mifune
—with Thanks to Akira Kurosawa
and the Toho La Brea Theater

Toshiro, you were so much more to me
than your movie star beauty,
though no one but you could look so appealing
in a ragged kimono, days without a bath,
scratching your head as you'd scrutinize the world.

Undeniably the best swordsman in Japan,
you took on single opponents or a gang of forty
with equal aplomb. And with that almost humane
efficiency, your sword moved faster than the eye,
each cut so quick and clean your victims fell
before they could utter a cry.

You were the perfect imperfect hero—
willing to defend a village of poor farmers
who'd repay you with a bowl of hot rice,
or selling yourself to the highest bidder,
you'd play crooked merchants against
conniving officials and noblemen.

It was your unfortunate karma
to be born into the rank of bushido warrior.
Each time you killed I knew you felt no satisfaction.
You were never the first to draw your sword.

All the women who watched you wanted you,
though you were awkward at romance. Not once
did I see you kiss a leading lady. Or lie
naked with her the night before battle.

You'd keep a girl waiting for months,
even years, like the lover who followed you
through the long 3-part saga, "The Legend of Musashi."

Toshiro, you were my first true film idol,
the Asian hero I could never find on the American screen.
I'll even admit you blessed those early years of marriage,
when my young husband and I spent Saturday nights
at the Toho La Brea. As the lights flashed back on,
my husband and every other Japanese man in the audience
would go home at least a few inches taller.

No one can forget you, Toshiro, in that brilliant duel
when you shifted your sword to reflect the sun,
the steel blade dazzling your enemy's eye.
And at the end of the story, as you slowly turned
your back and walked into the horizon,
that slightly bowlegged swagger
in your every step—no one came close.

The Shape of One Man's Breathing

: Saxophone Man

A woman who can't stop
watching the grip of your hands,
the fit of your lips and tongue
on the small reed mouthpiece,
wants you to play her
like your sax—pressed lightly
against chest, held
in a low curl along belly
and thighs, or tight
as you reach all the way
down, lift horn from hips,
legs kicking to a quick pulse,
fingers landing blindly,
groove to sweet groove.
She can't help staring,
and you keep wailing
this last chance
to blast your way back.

: Breath

Born two months early,
hardly enough breath
to keep you alive,
you surprised everyone
when you took up saxophone.

Sometimes at night you grasp
breath. Or after we make love,
inhale hard.

To survive you're learning
the shape of breath, a gift
I no longer take for granted.

You teach me about saxophone riffs
as we listen to Barbieri, Coltrane, Bird.
Every time you play your body
to mine, the refrain begins
from a brand new breath,
coming such a long way, wind
and me playing back,
sweet, unexpected notes
as we improvise together—
stretching the riff.

The Christening
—for Raul

From our bed we take time
to watch the late summer wind
as it rises, bringing in
cooler September days—

The wind pressing hard
against the sturdy
aspen, each white leaf
straining and trembling
on its stem—

As we witness
what shimmers in
the pale, almost sheer,
afternoon light, each small
body embracing its own.

Because the Rhythm of the Ballad Depends on the Bass: Acoustics of a Too Rapid Heart

more than ever I hear a slow bass line
the long space held between
each measured note I
watch for the fluid gesture
of practiced arms in caress
and fingers with a memory
strumming their way back in

I was never like young Dexter
slouching back in his chair
eyes dreamy and light
after he squeezes his saxophone for all
its sweetness so
new it lingers in the air

love comes later for me
a reward only earned
after too many years
or do I ask for too much
the most patient of hearts
and a hand which doesn't tire
calluses thick on fingertips
as the bassist plucks
a note so true it vibrates
through the body
comes into me like breath
returning
it is this low voice
I can hear through the others
repeating a slower rhythm

with each sure strum
I feel the long taut string
pulled all the way down
through my belly
how it echoes in me like an answer
delayed from too much longing
there's warming at the center
persistent wetness
in the small of my back

what resonates now
is the underside of a song
the sad steady beat it depends on
I feel my lover move inside me
slow and even
so my body can keep time
our rhythm unhurried
till my hips start to loosen
rising with his to a quicker beat
we keep this going as long as he can
but I could go on forever

maybe because love comes so late
I ground my passion
in this slower bass line
rendering myself to its full weight
or maybe it's as simple
as the long overdue knowing
that the man I love
after all is only a man

The Kumquat Seed Dancer
—based on a Butoh dance by Sankaijuku

Last night I saw
a man's body change into a woman's
making me forget
what I had always known as different.

The back is powdered white
head shaven
with legs bent
so knees are almost touching ground.

Her head turns slowly
arms extend
she turns as if someone far behind me
is calling.

Her spine doesn't move
as she looks back
palms and fingers lifted
mouth held open by a cry.

All at once
I knew her pain and wonder—
my own face
recognized in gesture.

Orchid

So stark
in the way it opens itself
to the world,
two petals spread full
like wings lifting
the flower from its blood
red center,
and a third lone petal grows,
smaller and heavy with vein,
its darkening rivulets
mar the petal's skin,
press against it
like the human veins
of a thinning hand, this
place where the orchid is most
and least lovely,
the place where it bleeds.

In a Room Named Shimmer
—for Ann

The woman folds underwear
her husband's t-shirts still
warm from the dryer
filling a wicker basket.

It is night outside but a sheer
white light resides here
an attention her hands
devote to the ordinary.

She has just washed her sweater
carefully reshaped the wet wool
to the width of her thin shoulders
the two arms extended
a girl feeling them rise in the wind.

Next to the window she keeps
a painting from Mexico
two red snakes with grins
and wings while angels
dance over their heads.

There's an intention in each detail
some purpose assigned
the word shimmer on her east wall
close by a small painted bird
resting almost unnoticed
until its wings begin to glisten
from some reflected light—
a life gleaned ever so slowly
each tiny glint more tremulous
and longing more insistent.

Spring Meal

I sit at the table.
Hear the chatter of women cooking.
Birds chirping. Surges of laughter.
I sip my coffee and read a poem.
Chew one word at a time,
filling me, syllable by syllable.
Tangerine. Tickle. Thermometer. Thigh.
I hear someone whisper. It could be you.
Or the voice I follow in sleep.
I listen to a story about hands—
hands which can map a face,
pressing palm
against bone and brow,
a finger tracing the curve
of a lip. Confirmation.
The gift which begins in gesture.
The man in my bed knows this
ritual of hands.
A necessity, he says, for the blind
to see what the heart remembers.

Out of Necessity

1

Waking up alone
has become my New Year's
tradition. So I run
for whatever fury
and release
this dislodged heart
can muster.
How I love the hard won sound
of my own painful exhaling.

2

I run like crazy the first five miles
push these stiff legs and arms
until I am nothing
but heart knocking
wildly and grunts
strung together
in tight airless breaths.

Then the exquisite rush
a moist heat rising
through body
the spine lengthens
lightness returning
to thighs and calves

And my heartbeat
so quiet
like the slowing
after orgasm.

3

On the walk home
I choose this street for its crimson blossoms
and citrus-scented leaves.

I like to time the steadying in my heart
with this view of the sky,
a warm winter blue.

4

I let my guard down.
No one's on the street but me.
It is New Year's day and this piece
of sidewalk opening to sky
is quite enough
for my meditation.
I don't want to let in
the sound of a car honking.
I resent its intrusion,
brace myself for the lewd
remarks and whistles
that often assault
a lone woman runner.
But something tells me
not to turn away from
this ancient Oldsmobile
with its huge purring
engine. I look into the dark
eyes of a young husband and wife,
two small children in the back.
They could be newcomers,
like the many poor immigrants

from Mexico. They smile
at me, pausing with intent,
as if we know each other.
And I wave back, sure
I've just seen angels.